US IMMIGRATION HISTORY POST 1870
DEMOGRAPHY & SETTLEMENT FOR KIDS

TIMELINES OF HISTORY FOR KIDS
6TH GRADE SOCIAL STUDIES

BABY PROFESSOR
EDUCATION KIDS

Speedy Publishing LLC
40 E. Main St. #1156
Newark, DE 19711
www.speedypublishing.com
Copyright 2018

All Rights reserved. No part of this book may be reproduced or used in any way or form or by any means whether electronic or mechanical, this means that you cannot record or photocopy any material ideas or tips that are provided in this book.

On this book, we're going to talk about the history of United States immigration after 1870. So, let's get right to it!

The United States is known as a "melting pot" because so many individuals from different countries have come to the United States to live. This mixture of various peoples and their cultures has made America strong. Everyone who lives in America today can trace their ancestry to immigrants unless they are directly descended from Native Americans. At times, United States policies have welcomed immigrants and at other times there have been restrictions prohibiting certain types of immigrants.

INTERNATIONAL GROUP OF HAPPY PEOPLE IN AMERICA

ENGLISH SETTLEMENT HOUSES

Timeline of Immigration to the United States

There were four distinct waves of immigration to the United States.

1607—The First Wave of Immigration

Beginning in 1607, settlers from England started coming to America. At this time, colonies were established as part of Great Britain. There was a steady flow of families from England as well as Scotland and Wales.

Immigrants from Germany and from the Netherlands also came during this first wave. The colonies they built ultimately caused tension with the Native American populations along the East Coast.

1820 to 1870—The Second Wave of Immigration

During this period of 50 years, over 7 million immigrants came to the United States. A third of these were people from Ireland. The potato famine in Ireland was one of the reasons these impoverished families fled to the United States. Many Irish people were seeking religious freedom and they wanted land that they could call their own.

IRISH PEASANTS STARVING DURING THE POTATO FAMINE

GERMAN IMMIGRANTS HEADING TO AMERICA

A large portion of this wave, also about a third, consisted of immigrants from Germany. They were generally more well off than the Irish. This group of immigrants settled in the cities of the East Coast and some moved to the Midwest in search of fertile farmland.

1845 to 1860—The Rise of Anti-Immigrant Sentiment

The "American Party" rose to influence during the mid-1800s. It became known as the "Know-Nothing Party" because when members were asked about their party affiliation they wouldn't admit it and instead said "I know nothing." The members were generally Protestants who disliked Roman Catholic immigrants.

ANTI-IMMIGRANT MEMBERS

DANIEL WEBSTER

They became powerful enough to support two candidates for president, Daniel Webster and also Millard Fillmore, who had been president previously. They were also responsible for several violent uprisings against immigrants who practiced Catholicism.

1848—80,000 Mexicans Become Citizens Overnight

When Mexico lost the Mexican-American War, a huge portion of their landmass became part of the United States. The Mexican people who lived in that region were immediately given United States citizenship. The region was turned into the state of California and its neighboring states of Nevada, Utah, and Arizona as well as sections of New Mexico and Colorado.

MEXICAN-AMERICAN WAR

AFRICAN AMERICAN FAMILY

1868—Citizenship is Granted to Every Person Who is Born in the US

The 13th Amendment to the Constitution made slavery illegal countrywide in 1865. In 1868, the 14th Amendment stated that all people born in the United States would be considered US citizens. The right of citizenship was also granted to African-Americans who were former slaves.

EUROPEAN IMMIGRANTS

1880 to 1920—The Third Wave of Immigration

Over these four decades, more than 24 million people came to the United States. The largest group consisted of Jewish people who were escaping persecution in Russia as well as immigrants from the eastern countries of Europe. Millions of Roman Catholics from Poland and countries in the southern portion of Europe also escaped to America.

EUROPEAN IMMIGRANTS ARRIVING AT ELLIS ISLAND

Many of these families came through Ellis Island, located in New York City. Another inspection station was located at Angel Island in San Francisco Bay. Thousands of immigrants from Asia came through this station beginning in 1910 and continuing through 1940.

1882—Congress Passes the Chinese Exclusion Act

Thousands of Chinese immigrants came to the US during the mid-1800s to find work during the Gold Rush in California. They helped to build the railroads during the time of the Industrial Revolution. However, there was a great deal of prejudice against them.

CHINESE PROSPECTORS WASHING GOLD IN A SLUICE BOX

CHINESE IMMIGRANTS IN SAN FRANCISCO

On 1882, Congress approved the Chinese Exclusion Act. Chinese people, both skilled as well as unskilled laborers, were banned from receiving work visas for a decade. This legislation continued to be in force until 1943.

1917—Congress Approves the Immigration Act

This legislation was brought about because of World War I and fears concerning keeping the United States secure. President Woodrow Wilson vetoed the Immigration Act, but the Congress still put it into force. The Act listed a group of undesirable people who wouldn't be allowed into the US. One of the groups listed were immigrants from Asian countries as well as Pacific Island countries.

WOODROW WILSON

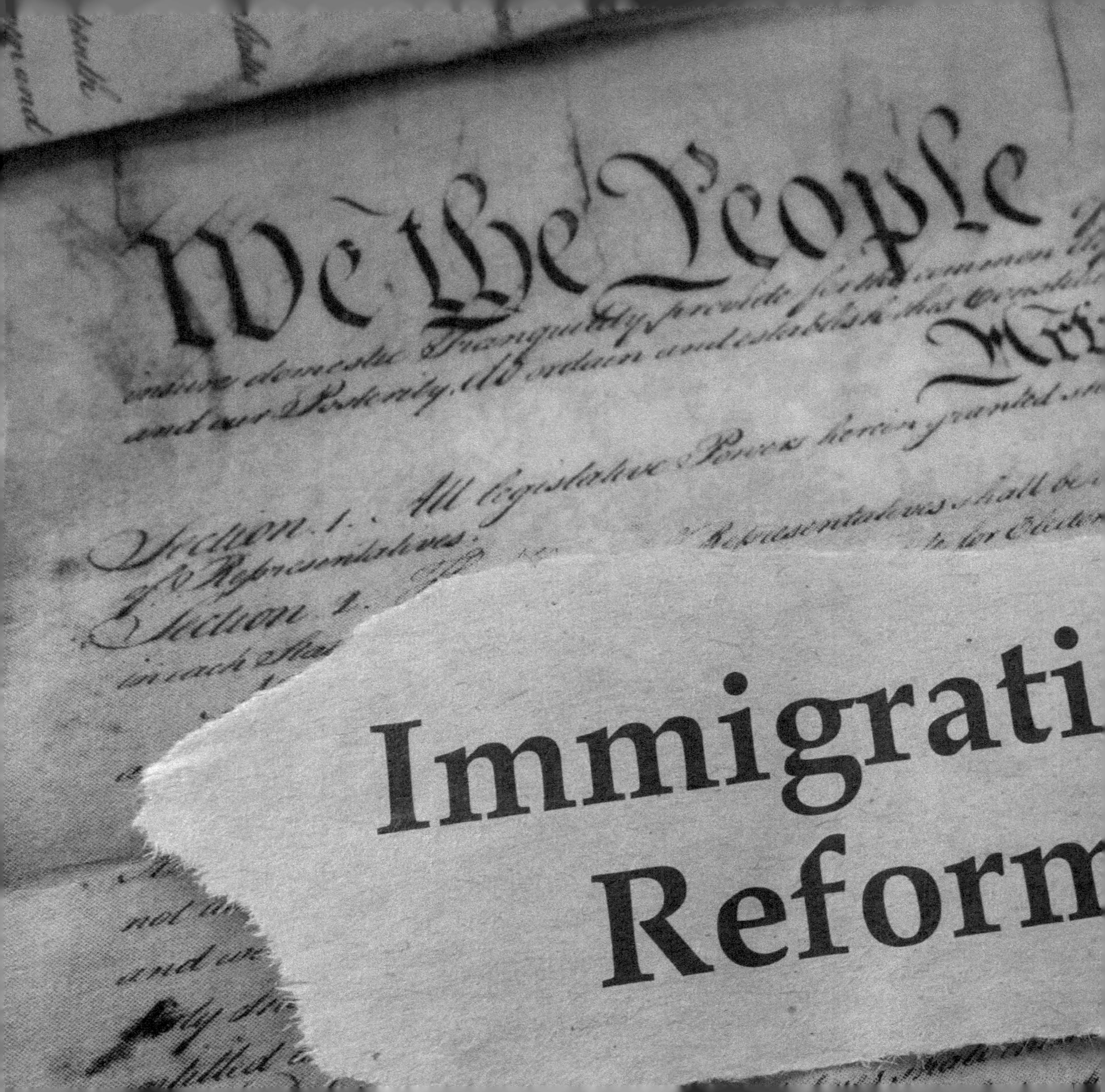
We the People
Immigrati
Reform

1921 to 1924—Strict Quotas Are Enacted

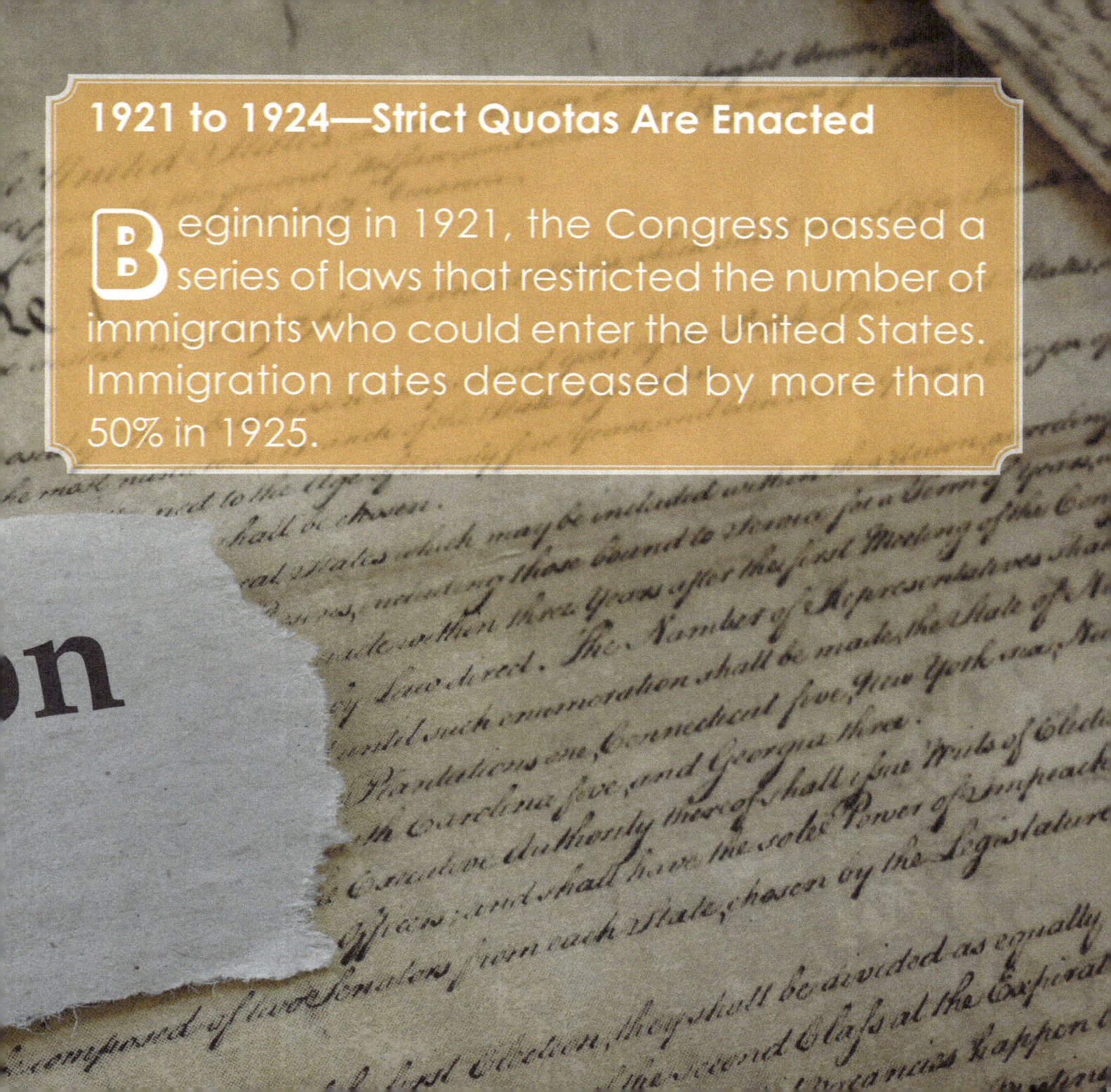

Beginning in 1921, the Congress passed a series of laws that restricted the number of immigrants who could enter the United States. Immigration rates decreased by more than 50% in 1925.

1948—Refugees from World War II Are Allowed to Enter

After World War II, the United States government allowed thousands of refugees from Europe to obtain a permanent home in the US. These were primarily people who had suffered persecution during Hitler's reign. Immigrants flocked to the US from Germany as well as Italy and Austria. Included in this group were about 80,000 Jewish people who had survived the war.

GERMAN REFUGEES FROM WORLD WAR II

COLD WAR FLAG

1952—The Immigration and Nationality Act of 1952

Congress approved the Immigration and Nationality Act in 1952 in response to the beginning of the Cold War. It eliminated most of the restrictions based on race. Most of the visas issued, about 85%, were given to people from the northern and western regions of Europe. Although the Act got rid of restrictions placed on Asians, since new visas were based on the previous quotas, there was still a restriction on the number of Asian people allowed into the US.

1965—The Fourth Wave of Immigration

On 1965, a revised Immigration and Nationality Act was approved. It changed the outdated quota process that was in place beginning in the 1920s. Instead of a quota based on the previous immigrant populations from various countries, this Act based the acceptance of immigrants due to their work skills and their family relationships with others who were already US citizens. The numbers of people coming to the United States every year almost doubled from 150,000 in the previous year to over 290,000. The fourth large wave of immigrants, who came from Mexico and South American countries, began.

MEXICANS ENTERING UNITED STATES AT THE IMMIGRATION STATION

RONALD REAGAN

1986—President Ronald Reagan Approves the Immigration Reform and Control Act

President Reagan approved the Immigration Reform and Control Act. This Act gave immigrants who were undocumented the opportunity to become citizens.

They had to meet these criteria:

- Not be accused of any crimes
- Show that they could read and write basic English
- Demonstrate a basic knowledge of US civics
- Have residence in the United States for four years or more continuously

AMERICAN CITIZENSHIP IMMIGRATION NATURALIZATION APPLICATION PROCESS

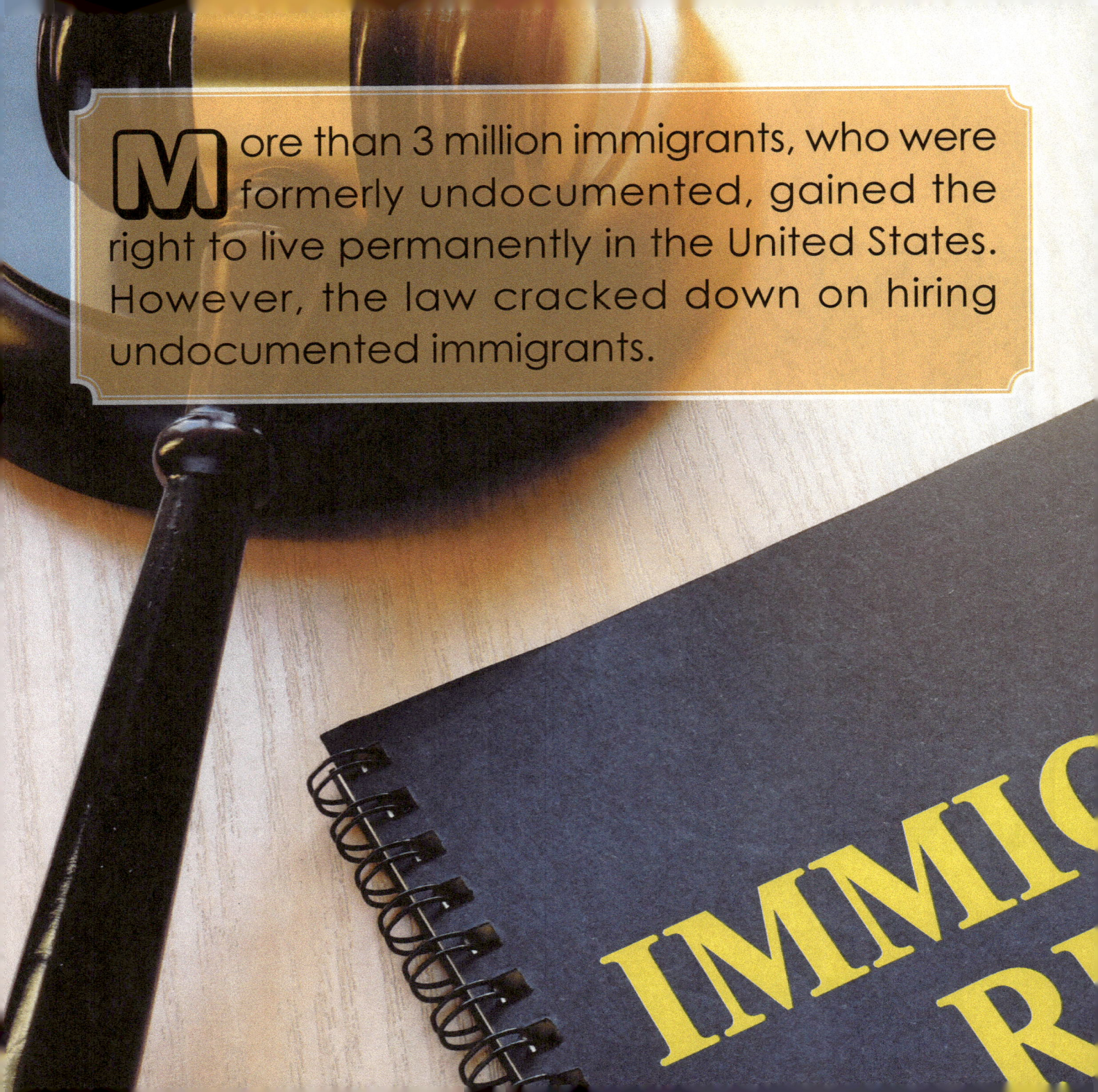

More than 3 million immigrants, who were formerly undocumented, gained the right to live permanently in the United States. However, the law cracked down on hiring undocumented immigrants.

...RATION
...FORM

1990—The Green Card Lottery is Established

The Immigration Act of 1990 made it possible for up to 700,000 immigrants to enter the US legally. Previously, only 500,000 were permitted. It also established a process for a visa system, commonly called the "green card lottery." This system provided 50 thousand visas every year to people coming from countries that had lower rates of immigration to the US. It also gave the president the power to take in immigrants who had suffered because of conflicts in their countries or natural disasters, such as earthquakes.

PERMANENT RESIDENT CARD OR GREEN CARD

ILLEGAL IMMIGRATION

1996—Crackdown on Illegal Immigration

President Bill Clinton signed a bill designed for immigration reform. This new law stated that if an immigrant was found to be in the United States illegally for over a year that he or she would be exiled from the US for more than a decade. During this time, there was an increase in the deportation of illegal immigrants. Deportation means that people are forced to leave the country.

2002—The Department of Homeland Security

After the tragedy of the terrorist attacks on 9/11, it was important for the United States to review its immigration policies. George W. Bush, who was president during the attacks, established a new department called the Department of Homeland Security. Within this new department, was a division called ICE, which stands for Immigration and Customs Enforcement.

GEORGE W. BUSH

US-MEXICAN BORDER IN ARIZONA, USA

Over the next ten years there was a significant increase in the deportation of illegal immigrants. The fence that divides the United States and Mexico was strengthened to ensure that people from other countries couldn't easily enter the US illegally.

2008 to 2012—Deportations Increase Dramatically

President Barack Obama cracked down on illegal immigrants. Over 1.5 million illegal immigrants were deported as part of the process to make the United States more secure from its enemies.

2012—Temporary Amnesty Issued by President Obama

President Obama issued temporary two-year work visas to young people who had come to the United States illegally.

BARACK OBAMA

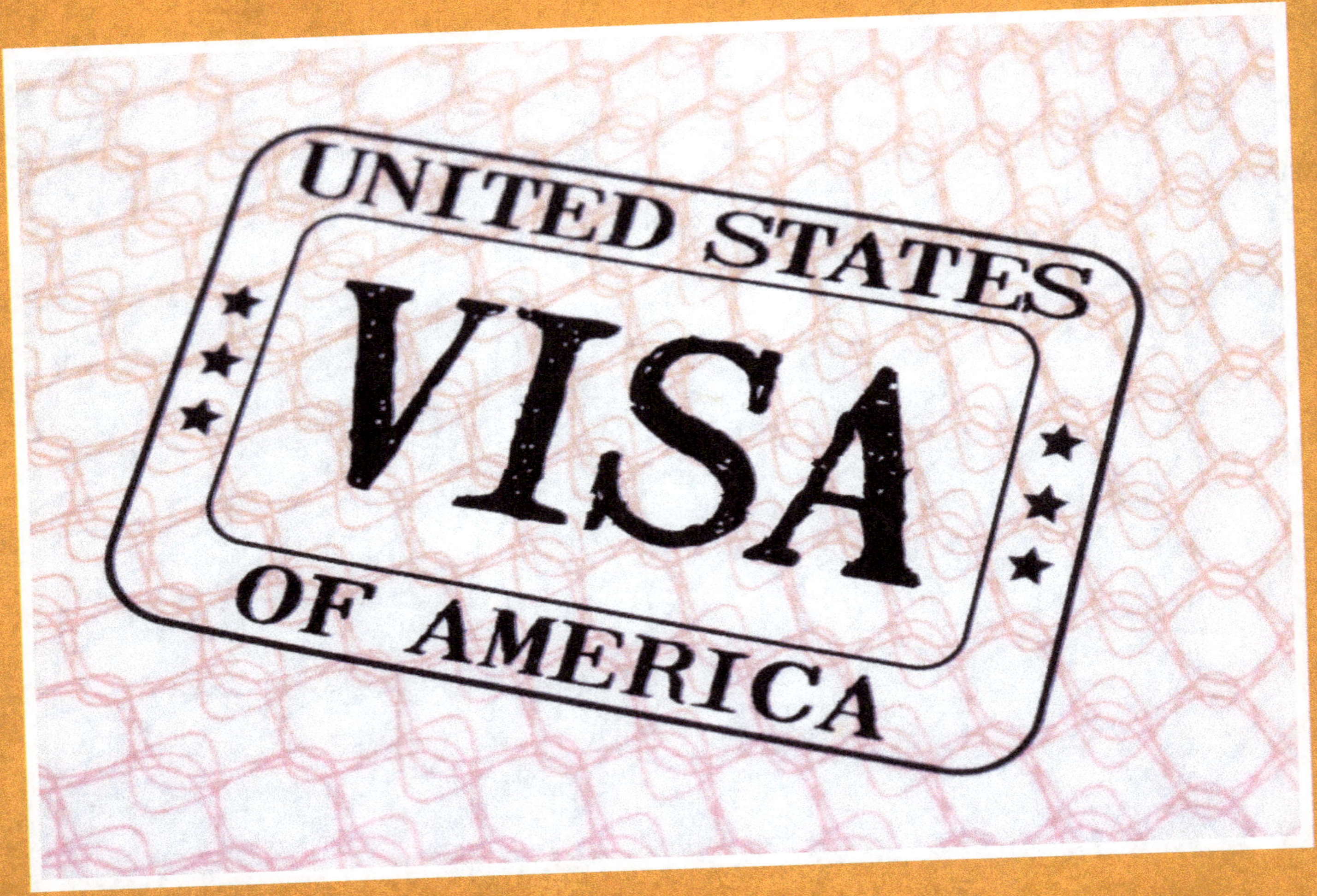
UNITED STATES
VISA
OF AMERICA

They had to fit certain criteria:

- Be 30 or less than 30 years of age
- Came to reside in the US before they were 16 years of age
- Lived in the US for a period of 5 years or more, continuously
- Were attending school or had graduated high school
- Had no criminal record

Over 1.7 million people were eligible for the two-year visas.

2017—President Donald Trump Cracks Down on Illegal Immigrants

During his campaign for president, Trump ignited anti-immigrant emotions. Some people believe that immigrants are responsible for increased crime and decreased jobs. He abolished some of Obama's policies and he promised to build a huge wall along the border with Mexico. He attempted to stop travelers from Muslim-led nations from entering the United States. Arrests of illegal immigrants increased dramatically during his first year in office.

TRUMP
DonaldJTrump.com
TRUMP
www.DonaldJTrump.com
MAKE AMERICA GREAT AGAIN!
Derry, New Hampshire

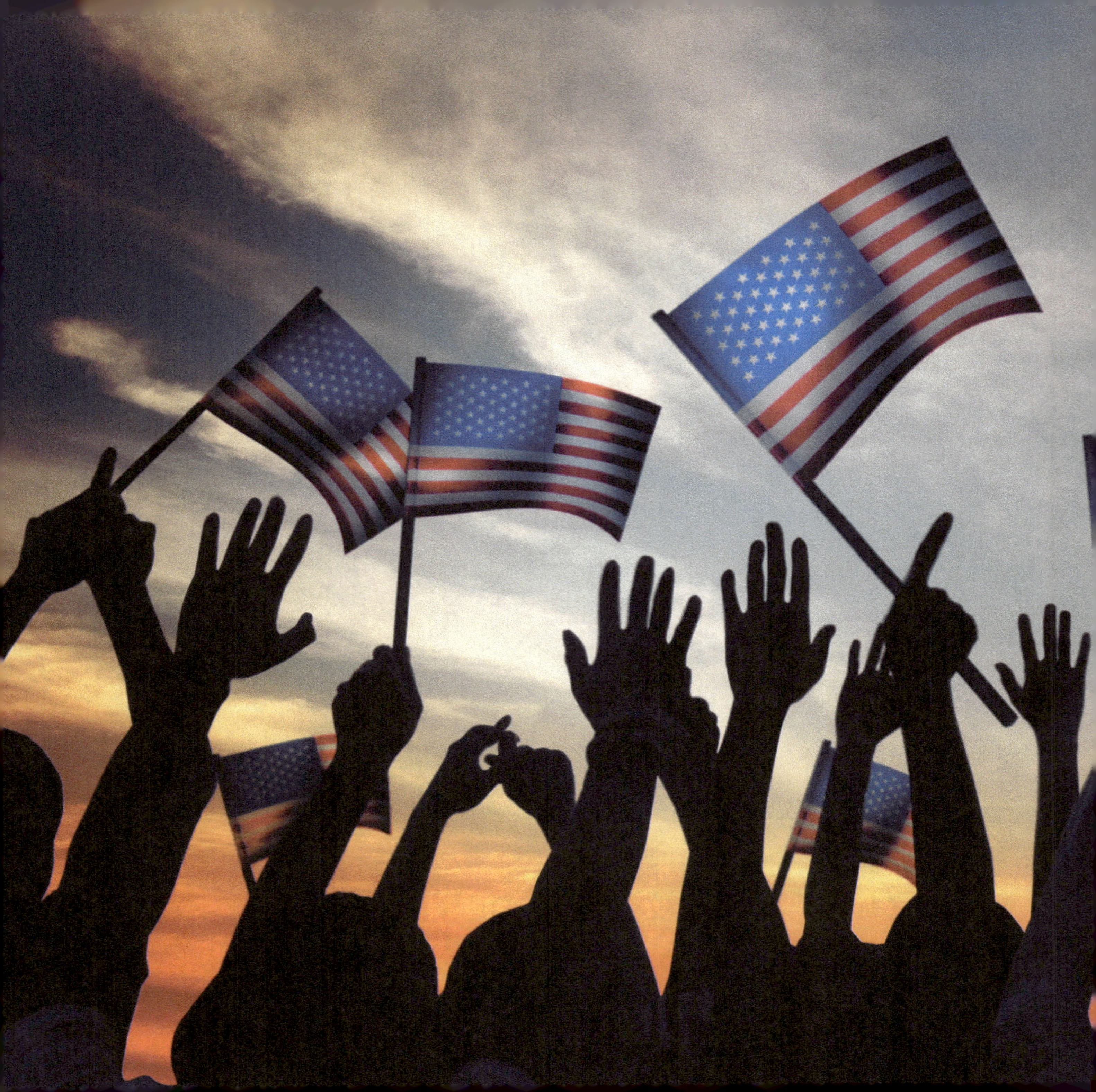

SUMMARY

Beginning in the year 1607, English settlers came to North America. They established colonies, which were part of the British Empire. Eventually, these immigrants fought for freedom and the United States was founded in 1776. From that time forward, people seeking freedom from persecution and poverty have come to the United States seeking refuge.

Now that you've read about the history of US immigration after 1870 you may want to read about the United States economy in the mid-1800s in the Baby Professor book, U.S. Economy in the Mid-1800s - Historical Timelines for Kids | American Historian Guide for Children | 5th Grade Social Studies.

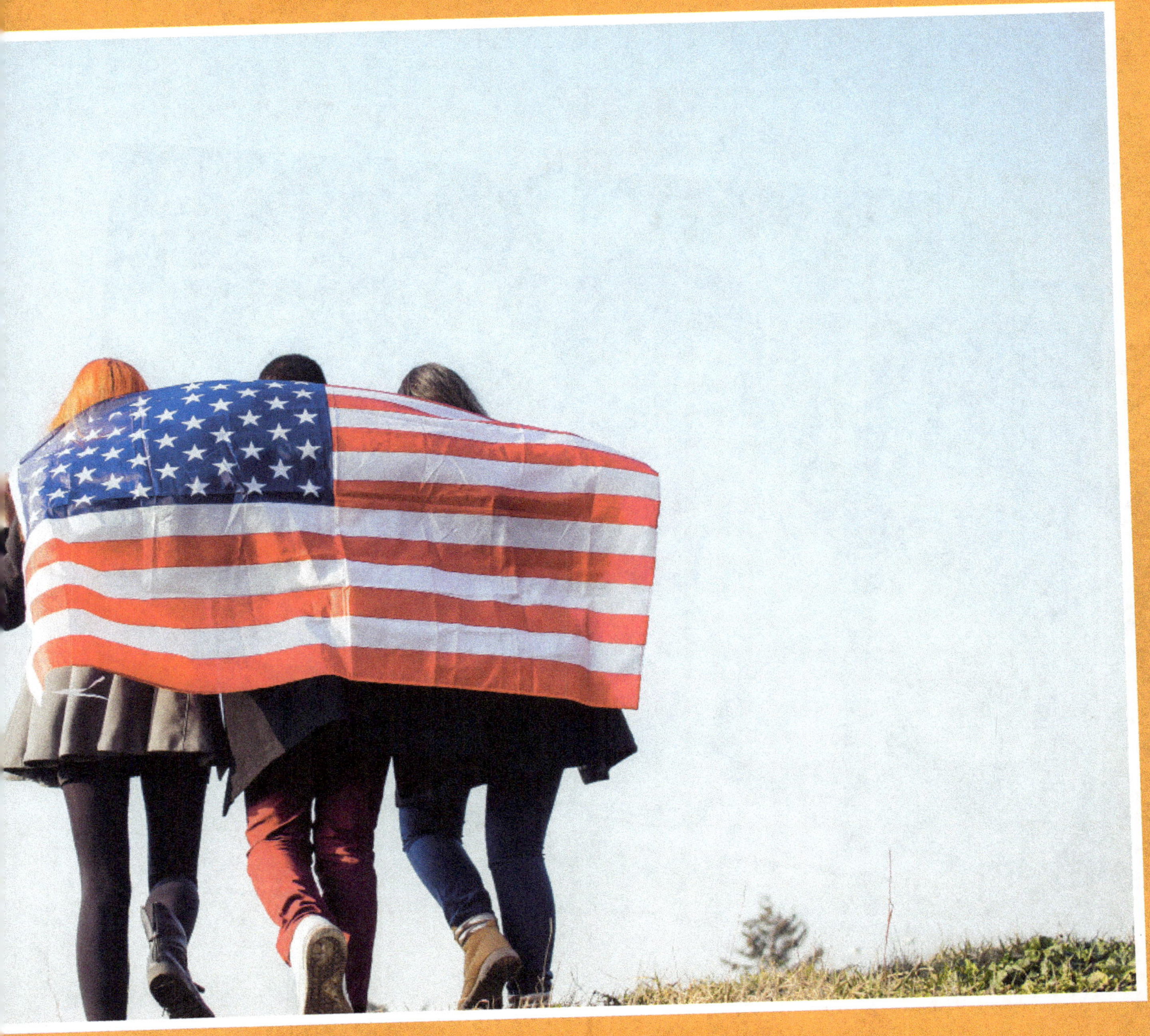

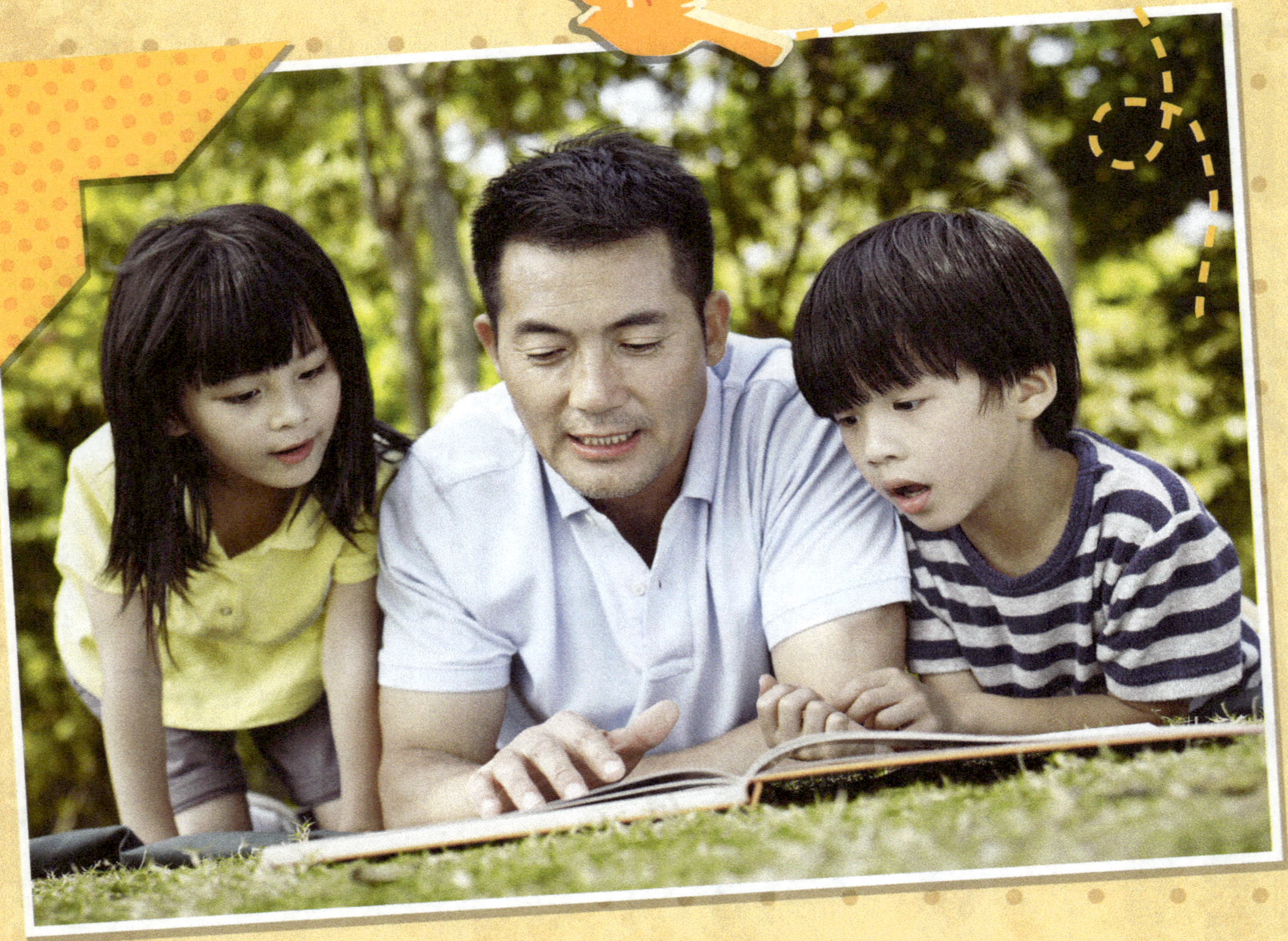

Visit

BABY PROFESSOR
EDUCATION KIDS

www.BabyProfessorBooks.com

to download Free Baby Professor eBooks
and view our catalog of new and exciting
Children's Books